LET'S
see

Ancient Egypt

by Cynthia Klingel and Robert B. Noyed

Content Adviser: Dr. Jennifer Houser Wegner, Research Scientist,
Egyptian Section, University of Pennsylvania Museum, Philadelphia

Reading Adviser: Dr. Linda D. Labbo, Department of Reading Education,
College of Education, The University of Georgia

Let's See Library
Compass Point Books
Minneapolis, Minnesota

Compass Point Books
3722 West 50th Street, #115
Minneapolis, MN 55410

Visit Compass Point Books on the Internet at *www.compasspointbooks.com* or e-mail your
request to *custserv@compasspointbooks.com*

Cover: Great Sphinx, Giza, Egypt

Photographs ©: PhotoDisc, cover; Archivo Iconografico, S.A./Corbis, 6; The Newberry Library/Stock Montage,
8; North Wind Picture Archives, 10, 16, 20; Stock Montage, 12; Réunion des Musées Nationaux/Art Resource,
N.Y., 14; Digital Stock, 18.

Editors: E. Russell Primm, Emily J. Dolbear, and Pam Rosenberg
Photo Researcher: Svetlana Zhurkina
Photo Selector: Linda S. Koutris
Designer: Melissa Voda
Cartographer: XNR Productions, Inc.

Library of Congress Cataloging-in-Publication Data
Klingel, Cynthia Fitterer.
  Ancient Egypt / by Cynthia Klingel and Robert B. Noyed.
    p. cm. — (Let's see library)
  Includes bibliographical references and index.
  ISBN 0-7565-0291-8 (hardcover)
    1. Egypt—Civilization—To 332 B.C.—Juvenile literature. [1. Egypt—Civilization—To 332 B.C.] I. Noyed,
Robert B. II. Title. III. Series.
  DT61 .K48 2002
  932'.01—dc21
                                                            2002003037

Table of Contents

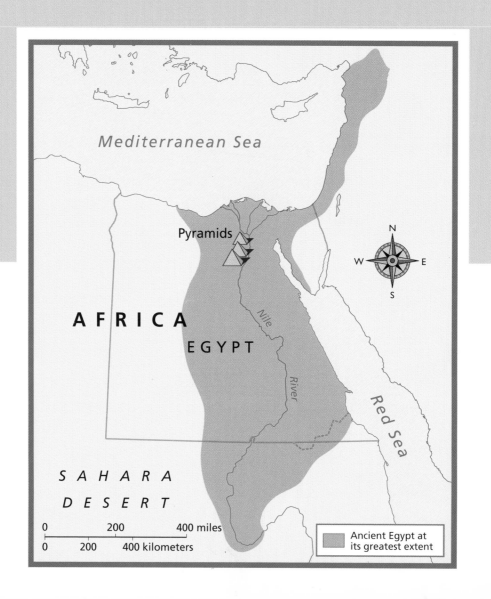

Mediterranean Sea

Pyramids

AFRICA

EGYPT

Nile

River

Red Sea

SAHARA
DESERT

N
W   E
S

0	200	400 miles

0	200	400 kilometers

Ancient Egypt at
its greatest extent

What Was Ancient Egypt?

Ancient Egypt was a country in the northeastern corner of Africa. The modern country of Egypt covers much of the same area. Most of the land is desert. The Nile River runs through the middle of the country. The kingdom of a united ancient Egypt started about 5,000 years ago. It lasted almost 3,000 years.

Ancient Egypt was divided into two areas. One area was called *deshret,* meaning "red land." The sand there was red. The land along the Nile River was called *kemet,* meaning "black land." The soil there was rich, dark, and good for growing crops.

◄ *The Nile River ran through ancient Egypt.*

Who Were the Ancient Egyptians?

The ancient Egyptians probably looked like today's Egyptians. They had black hair, dark eyes, and their skin was a reddish brown color. Most Egyptians were farmers. They lived simply. They wore clothes made of rough cloth. A few Egyptians were rich. They wore clothes made of **linen.**

Most Egyptian men and women wore makeup around their eyes. This makeup was called *kohl.* They thought it made their eyes look nice. It also protected their eyes from the bright sun. Rich people wore jewelry made of gold and silver. Working people wore jewelry made of clay or bone.

◄ *This sculpture of Queen Nefertiti shows how Egyptians wore kohl around their eyes.*

What Was Important to the Ancient Egyptians?

Ancient Egyptians believed in life after death. They believed they would live forever in their next life. The Egyptians spent a lot of time and money building their tombs.

The ancient Egyptians **preserved** the bodies of dead people. Then the bodies were wrapped in layers of linen. These preserved bodies are called mummies. The mummies were placed in tombs and buried with food, clothing, tools, and jewelry. The Egyptians believed people would need these objects in the next life. Mummies from ancient Egypt are in many museums today.

◄ *A mummy inside its case*

What Kind of Government Did They Have?

Ancient Egypt was ruled by a king called a *pharaoh*. When the pharaoh died, his **successor** became the next pharaoh. The pharaoh's son was usually his successor. Only a few women ruled ancient Egypt. The pharaoh made all the decisions for the people of Egypt. The pharaoh lived in a palace.

The Egyptians sometimes went to war. They were brave and strong warriors. Soldiers used spears, axes, and clubs as well as bows and arrows. They usually fought on foot. After 1500 B.C., the ancient Egyptians used **chariots** and horses. Sometimes the pharaoh led the soldiers into battle.

◄ The crowning of a pharaoh

Why Was the Nile River So Valuable?

The Nile River brought life to ancient Egypt. Every year the river flooded over its banks. When the waters went down, a layer of rich soil remained on the ground. This soil was excellent for growing crops. The Nile also provided fish for the Egyptians to eat.

The god of floods was named Hapy. The Egyptians believed Hapy flooded the Nile each year. Hapy was sometimes shown painted green and holding a platter of food. The color green represented the waves of the river. The platter of food represented the harvests Hapy provided.

◄ *An ancient Egyptian illustration shows hunting, fishing, and harvesting.*

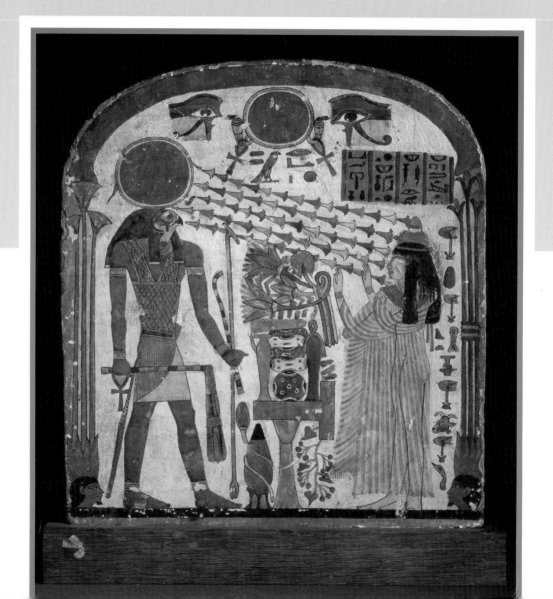

What Was the Religion of Ancient Egypt?

Ancient Egyptians had many gods and goddesses. They worshiped them in their own homes. Only priests and the pharaoh could enter the temples. One of the most important gods was Re, the sun god. The Egyptians believed that the pharaoh was a god, too. He was called the son of Re.

Sometimes the gods and goddesses looked like animals. Sometimes they looked like humans with animal heads! Many people wore special charms to honor a certain god or goddess. Bastet was an important goddess who protected the home. She was often shown as a cat.

◀ *An Egyptian woman worships one of her gods, Re-Horakty.*

What Kind of Work Did They Do?

Farming was the most common work in ancient Egypt. Egyptians also worked as craftspeople. They made pottery, jewelry, and furniture. Many skilled craftspeople worked for the government. They built temples, palaces, and royal tombs. Some people worked as bakers, weavers, and artists.

The scribes had one of the most important jobs in ancient Egypt. Most Egyptians could not read or write. So it was the scribes' job to write letters and keep records for the Egyptian people. Some boys went to a special school to learn to read and write. They would be scribes someday.

◄ *A scribe keeps records for the pharaoh and others.*

What Arts Were Important in Ancient Egypt?

Paintings and literature were important to the ancient Egyptians. Egyptian tombs and temples are covered with pictures and words. Some show the pharaoh. Some show gods and goddesses. Others show the daily life of an average person. Egyptian poems and stories were written in **hieroglyphs** on scrolls of **papyrus.**

The design of Egyptian buildings is a form of art. The pyramids were built to be tombs for the pharaohs. The Egyptians also built beautiful temples. Many of these buildings are still standing today.

◀ *The base of the Temple of Ramses shows examples of hieroglyphs.*

How Do We Remember Ancient Egypt?

Most people are still interested in ancient Egypt. **Archaeologists** help us learn more about ancient Egypt. They study the people of ancient civilizations and how they lived.

Archaeologists study pyramids, temples, and tombs. Mummies and the treasures buried with them help us learn more, too. They tell us how ancient Egyptians lived. We also learn about them by reading their stories. The stories tell us what the people thought of life and death. Each day, archaeologists work to bring us more information about Egypt and other ancient civilizations.

◄ *The Sphinx at Giza is one of the world's greatest monuments.*

Glossary

archaeologists—scientists who study people, places, and things of the past

chariots—two-wheeled carts pulled by horses

hieroglyphs—writing made up of pictures

linen—a fine, thin cloth made from the fibers of the flax plant

papyrus—paper made from the stems of water plants

preserved—kept from decaying

successor—the person next in line for a position

Did You Know?

• Cleopatra was the last queen of Egypt but she was not an Egyptian. She was a member of a Greek family.

• The biggest pyramid built by the ancient Egyptians is called the Great Pyramid. It stands about fifty stories tall.

• One of Egypt's most famous tombs is the tomb of Tutankhamen, or "King Tut." He became pharaoh when he was about nine years old and died when he was about eighteen. His tomb is filled with gold and other treasures.

Want to Know More?

At the Library

Cole, Joanna, and Bruce Degen (illustrator). *Ancient Egypt*. New York: Scholastic, 2001.

Fisher, Leonard Everett. *The Gods and Goddesses of Ancient Egypt*. New York: Holiday House, 1999.

Osborne, Will, Mary Pope Osborne, and Sal Murdocca (illustrator). *Mummies and Pyramids*. New York: Random House, 2001.

On the Web

Ancient Egypt

http://www.ancientegypt.co.uk/menu.html

To learn more about life in ancient Egypt through stories and games

Ancient Egypt Webquest

http://www.iwebquest.com/egypt/ancientegypt.htm

To find fun activities and a list of books that will help you learn more about ancient Egypt

Rosetta Stone

http://www.clemusart.com/archive/pharaoh/rosetta/index.html

To learn more about ancient Egypt through art projects and coloring pages

Through the Mail

The Embassy of the Arab Republic of Egypt

3521 International Court, N.W.
Washington, DC 20008
202/895-5400
To write for more information about the country of Egypt

On the Road

The Field Museum

1400 South Lake Shore Drive
Chicago, IL 60605
312/922-9410
To view the exhibit *Inside Ancient Egypt*

Index

About the Authors

Cynthia Klingel has worked as a high school English teacher and an elementary schoolteacher. She is currently the curriculum director for a Minnesota school district. Cynthia Klingel lives with her family in Mankato, Minnesota.

Robert B. Noyed started his career as a newspaper reporter. Since then, he has worked in school communications and public relations at the state and national level. Robert B. Noyed lives with his family in Brooklyn Center, Minnesota.